HOUSE

CW00524004

European Union Committee

20th Report of Session 2007–08

Current Developments in European Defence Policy

Report with Evidence

Ordered to be printed 15 July 2008 and published 1 August 2008

Published by the Authority of the House of Lords

London : The Stationery Office Limited
£6.50

HL Paper 145

The European Union Committee

The European Union Committee is appointed by the House of Lords "to consider European Union documents and other matters relating to the European Union". The Committee has seven Sub-Committees which are:

Economic and Financial Affairs, and International Trade (Sub-Committee A)
Internal Market (Sub-Committee B)
Foreign Affairs, Defence and Development Policy (Sub-Committee C)
Environment and Agriculture (Sub-Committee D)
Law and Institutions (Sub-Committee E)
Home Affairs (Sub-Committee F)
Social and Consumer Affairs (Sub-Committee G)

Our Membership

The Members of the European Union Committee are:

Lord Blackwell
Baroness Cohen of Pimlico
Lord Dykes
Lord Freeman
Lord Grenfell (Chairman)
Lord Harrison
Baroness Howarth of Breckland
Lord Jopling
Lord Kerr of Kinlochard
Lord Maclennan of Rogart

Lord Mance
Lord Plumb
Lord Powell of Bayswater
Lord Roper
Lord Sewel
Baroness Symons of Vernham Dean
Lord Tomlinson
Lord Wade of Chorlton
Lord Wright of Richmond

The Members of the Sub-Committee which carried out this inquiry (Foreign Affairs, Defence and Development Policy, Sub-Committee C) are:

Lord Anderson of Swansea
Lord Boyce
Lord Chidgey
Lord Crickhowell
Lord Hamilton of Epsom
Lord Hannay of Chiswick

Lord Jones
Lord Roper (Chairman)
Lord Selkirk of Douglas
Lord Swinfen
Baroness Symons of Vernham Dean
Lord Truscott

Information about the Committee

The reports and evidence of the Committee are published by and available from The Stationery Office. For information freely available on the web, our homepage is:
http://www.parliament.uk/parliamentary_committees/lords_eu_select_committee.cfm
There you will find many of our publications, along with press notices, details of membership and forthcoming meetings, and other information about the ongoing work of the Committee and its Sub-Committees, each of which has its own homepage.

General Information

General information about the House of Lords and its Committees, including guidance to witnesses, details of current inquiries and forthcoming meetings is on the internet at
http://www.parliament.uk/about_lords/about_lords.cfm

Contacts for the European Union Committee

Contact details for individual Sub-Committees are given on the website.
General correspondence should be addressed to the Clerk of the European Union Committee, Committee Office, House of Lords, London, SW1A OPW
The telephone number for general enquiries is 020 7219 5791.
The Committee's email address is euclords@parliament.uk

CONTENTS

Oral Evidence

Mr Andrew Mathewson, Director for Policy on International Organisations, Ministry of Defence; Mr Robert Regan, Director, International Relations Group, Defence Equipment & Support, Ministry of Defence; Mr Ian Hall, Head of Research Collaboration, Ministry of Defence
Oral evidence, 26 June 2008   1

NOTE: In the text of the report:
(Q) refers to a question in oral evidence

Current Developments in European Defence Policy

REPORT

1. In this Report we make available, for the information of the House, the oral evidence given to Sub-Committee C (Foreign Affairs, Defence and Development Policy) by Mr Andrew Mathewson, Director for Policy on International Organisations, Mr Robert Regan, Director, International Relations Group, Defence Equipment and Support and Mr Ian Hall, Head of Research Collaboration, Ministry of Defence, on 26 June 2008.

2. Key topics in the evidence are:

   - the European Defence Agency (EDA) budget and European defence spending, value for money issues (QQ 1, 2, 5–7, 9, 18–20);

   - the size and focus of the EDA Work Programme and the desirability of a linkage between the Financial Framework and the Work Programme (QQ 1–3);

   - the future of the EDA, including Permanent Structured Cooperation, after the Irish "No" vote on the Lisbon Treaty (QQ 3, 4, 43);

   - the issues surrounding the UK's non-participation in projects in the Joint Investment Programme on research into Innovative Concepts and Emerging Technologies and the Force Protection Joint Investment Programme (QQ 10–16);

   - Research and Development in Europe including the relative contributions of different European nations (QQ 17, 18);

   - discussion of the value of collaboration between groups of countries with special interests or expertise (QQ 19, 20);

   - the EDA's and European Commission's work on the European Defence Technological and Industrial Base strategy (EDTIB); the competitive defence industry in Europe (Q 21);

   - defence sales in the USA (Q 22);

   - the UK's Defence Industrial Strategy (Q 22);

   - the need for global procurement in order to acquire the best capability and interoperability (QQ 25–27);

   - the availability of helicopters for demanding operations (QQ 9, 28);

   - the European Commission's Defence Package, including the Directive on the coordination of procedures for the award of certain public works contracts or defence works contracts; opening up markets (QQ 29, 30, 32–39);

   - problems associated with the operation of Article 296 and the Code of Conduct, including the role of the European Court of Justice (QQ 29–31, 36, 37);

   - classified projects and the definition of the security sector (QQ 34–38);

- preparations for Battlegroups and the availability of troops in the light of competing demands (QQ 40, 41);

- the possible use of Battlegroups for the evacuation of British citizens in a crisis (Q 42).

APPENDIX 1: SUB-COMMITTEE C (FOREIGN AFFAIRS, DEFENCE AND DEVELOPMENT POLICY)

The Members of the Sub-Committee which conducted this Inquiry were:

> Lord Anderson of Swansea
> Lord Boyce
> Lord Chidgey
> Lord Crickhowell
> Lord Hamilton of Epsom
> Lord Hannay of Chiswick
> Lord Jones
> Lord Roper (Chairman)
> Lord Selkirk of Douglas
> Lord Swinfen
> Baroness Symons of Vernham Dean
> Lord Truscott

Declaration of Interests

A full list of Members' interests can be found in the Register of Lords' Interests:

http://www.publications.parliament.uk/pa/ld/ldreg.htm

APPENDIX 2: RECENT REPORTS

Recent Reports from the EU Select Committee

Evidence from the Ambassador of the Federal Republic of Germany on the German Presidency (10th Report, Session 2006–07, HL Paper 56)

The Commission's Annual Policy Strategy for 2008 (23rd Report, Session 2006–07, HL Paper 123)

Further Enlargement of the EU: Follow-up Report (24th Report, Session 2006–07, HL Paper 125)

Evidence from the Minister for Europe on the June European Union Council and the 2007 Inter-Governmental Conference (28th Report, Session 2006–07, HL Paper 142)

Evidence from the Ambassador of Portugal on the Priorities of the Portuguese Presidency (29th Report, session 2006–07, HL Paper 143)

The EU Reform Treaty: work in progress (35th Report, Session 2006–07, HL Paper 180)

Annual Report 2007 (36th Report, Session 2006–07, HL Paper 181)

The Treaty of Lisbon: an impact assessment (10th Report, Session 2007–08, HL Paper 62)

Priorities of the European Union: evidence from the Minister for Europe and the Ambassador of Slovenia (11th Report, Session 2007–08, HL Paper 73)

Session 2007–2008 Reports prepared by Sub-Committee C

Current Developments in European Foreign Policy: the EU and Africa (4th Report, HL Paper 32)

Current Developments in European Defence Policy (8th Report, HL Paper 59)

Current Developments in European Foreign Policy (12th Report, HL Paper 75)

The European Union and Russia (14th Report, HL Paper 98)

Current Developments in European Foreign Policy: Burma (16th Report, HL Paper 118)

Session 2006–2007 Reports prepared by Sub-Committee C

Current Developments in European Defence Policy (1st Report, HL Paper 17)

Current Developments in European Foreign Policy (16th Report, HL Paper 76)

The EU and the Middle East Peace Process (26th Report, HL Paper 132)

Current Developments in European Foreign Policy: Kosovo (32nd Report, HL Paper 154)

Current Developments in European Defence Policy (34th Report, HL Paper 161)

Current Developments in European Foreign Policy (38th Report, HL Paper 183)

Minutes of Evidence

THURSDAY 26 JUNE 2008

Present	Anderson of Swansea, L	Hannay of Chiswick, L
	Boyce, L	Jones, L
	Chidgey, L	Roper, L (Chairman)
	Crickhowell, L	Selkirk of Douglas, L
	Hamilton of Epsom, L	

Examination of Witnesses

Witnesses: MR ANDREW MATHEWSON, Director, Policy on International Organisations, MR ROBERT REGAN, Director, International Relations Group, Defence Equipment & Support and MR IAN HALL, Head of Research Collaboration, Ministry of Defence gave evidence.

Chairman: Mr Mathewson, we are very pleased to see you again, together with Mr Regan and Mr Hall. As I think you know, apart from the questions on the EDA Steering Board meeting, we would also like to raise some questions with you on the Commission Defence Package which is obviously before us and which we need to consider, and then finally move on to one or two questions on the European Security Strategy and Battlegroups.

Q1 *Lord Boyce:* This is an area we have covered on previous occasions and a concern about whether the EDA can function as efficiently as it might without having a good feel for its long-term financial position. Previously the EDA have stated that you have resisted adoption of a three-year financial framework. Do you think the government might be able to agree a three-year framework in 2009? Do you think that our position is understood by some of the other Member States, that we could be conceived as holding back the EDA from being able to spread it wings properly and knowing where it is going in three years' time rather than working on an annual-type basis?
Mr Mathewson: I do not think it is quite fair to say we resisted the setting up of the three-year framework in principle. What we have is disagreement on the scale of the three-year framework each time we have tried to set it but in principle we would be happy to see a three-year framework set. We have been making the case for a clearer connection between a three-year financial framework and a three-year work programme. At the moment we have a sense that the work programme is not well based, it is not well matched against the resources and we would like to see a longer three-year perspective that matched resourcing to the work expected. At the moment we do not sense there is a good connection between

those two but we will still try to work with them to develop that perspective on the basis of a better understanding of the work programme. That view is shared by a number of other countries. There is clearly a range of views about the rate at which the EDA should grow and I will not pretend that we are not amongst those countries who see it growing rather more slowly than some of the others but most countries do want to see a better articulated work programme and financial perspective so that they can see how the resources are being allocated.

Q2 *Lord Boyce:* Given this problem has been running for many months, probably over a year or so, they must know the particular concern we and other countries have yet they do not have a work programme. I find it difficult to believe that they have not sorted this problem out yet.
Mr Mathewson: They do have a work programme but we cannot see when we look at the work programme the connection to the resource. There is no evident connection between the resources they are asking for and the work programme they are setting out to undertake, which for us is frustrating because it means we are having a discussion about the budget somewhat in a vacuum. We would rather have a good connection between the work programme and the budget so we can get into the question of prioritisation. How far up this work programme can we afford to spend and where do we draw the line? We cannot get at that discussion. Even those who want the more generous budget would like to see that because they would see it as a way of arguing for more resources. Like you, we are frustrated that the Agency has not been able to make this connection between resourcing and work programme. We expressed our frustration at that last week.

Q3 *Lord Anderson of Swansea:* There is an impression that we had an ideological concern about a three-year budget and what you are saying is it is a pragmatic one in relation to a mismatch between the work programme and resources. Is this a view which is, in your judgment, gaining? Is there likely to be agreement within a reasonable period, next year or so, on the three-year programme? Clearly we have an image problem in that many think of us as minimalist in our view of what the EDA can do. How do you rebut that?

Mr Mathewson: We are cautious rather than minimalist is the word I would use. We are investing a significant resource in the EDA and we want to see it delivering results. We believe at the moment that the EDA is spreading its wings too far and is trying to do too much. The work programme is too big and it would be better focusing it down trying to do rather fewer projects rather better. That is where we would like to see the Agency develop. We are not going to set a three-year framework this year. The Ministers agreed in the Steering Board in May not to try to set a three-year framework this year. That was partly a reflection on the difficulties we had setting it last year in identifying the scale of the programme not the principle of whether we should have one. Partly it is a reflection of some uncertainty about what the Agency's role might be. The Lisbon Treaty, if it were introduced, would introduce permanent structured co-operation which might have some implications for the role of the Agency. There was a degree of uncertainty about what the Agency might do over the next three years. Ministers agreed in their Steering Board in May to recommend to the Council that we do not try to set a three-year financial perspective this year but we will be trying in 2009 for the three years after that.

Q4 *Lord Anderson of Swansea:* Uncertainties following the Irish No will presumably continue those difficulties in relation to an agreed programme.

Mr Mathewson: Yes. As long as the question of whether we are going to implement the Lisbon Treaty and try to undertake permanent structured co-operation is open, then there will be a degree of a question mark over the precise role of the Agency.

Q5 *Lord Hamilton of Epsom:* If the money was found for this budget where would it come from?

Mr Mathewson: The MoD finances the UK contribution to the EDA.

Q6 *Lord Hamilton of Epsom:* We are talking about European nation states' defence budgets which have been in constant decline and the chances of finding extra money seem to be as near nil as makes no difference.

Mr Mathewson: Certainly budgets are in decline. We checked and established that every other country funds the Agency from the MoD rather than general Community funds. Yes, I think it is difficult for us to understand from our perspective, with heavy operational pressure and heavy pressure on the defence budget to deliver against current operations, the priorities which some others attach to increasing the scale of the size of the EDA's budget. We are not against increasing the size of the EDA budget.

Q7 *Lord Hamilton of Epsom:* As long as somebody else does it.

Mr Mathewson: But on the basis of a value for money consideration that we are going to get something out of it. Our approach to the scale of the budget will be: is this the best way to spend defence resources. We hope eventually the Agency can develop such that they can show to us this is a good way to spend defence resources and then we can make genuine business case decisions on increasing the size of the budget rather than the decision in principle that this is good for Europe that we are sometimes led towards at the moment.

Q8 *Lord Hannay of Chiswick:* Presumably, in that case, if all 27 Member States asked the same question you asked none would ever be agreed?

Mr Mathewson: I do not quite understand the question.

Q9 *Lord Hannay of Chiswick:* If all 27 Member States asked and answered the question in the way you proposed it, is this for our national good or for the collective good, they would presumably all get the answer that you get now: no.

Mr Mathewson: Not necessarily. Certainly all defence capability in Europe is developed by Member States rather than by the institution. We can certainly see ways in which Member States co-operating through the Agency can get best value for money in developing new capability. For example, we think the Agency might have a sensible role to play in developing helicopter capability, which is an area you might come back to later. It is easier to see these judgments have been formed on the basis of small coalitions of countries coming together on the basis of a common objective than on the basis of a presumed genuine increase in the level of funding.

Q10 *Lord Hamilton of Epsom:* In his letter of the 19 May 2008 the Secretary of State for Defence explained that the UK would not be participating in the Joint Investment Programme on research into innovative concepts and emerging technologies. Given that this programme came out of the Hampton Court initiative launched under the UK presidency in 2005, is the UK being consistent in deciding not to join in and would the programme benefit from the UK's participation and considerable expertise in this area?

Mr Hall: First of all, we would not recognise that it came directly out of the Hampton Court initiative as the precise subject matter certainly occurred a year or two after that. More importantly, the general principle of the Joint Investment Programme was something which was slightly anterior to the Hampton Court agenda and was essentially looking at central funding for R&T in Europe which is something, as I will explain in a minute, there are some difficulties with. We would not say that by not participating in ICET we are not fulfilling our part of the Hampton Court agenda by any means at all as it was far, far broader than just this one initiative on which it has been interrupted. In terms of the Joint Investment Programme, specifically in the ICET (Innovative Concepts and Emerging Technologies), there are two issues. Firstly, rather like the Force Protection Investment Programme, when we actually looked at the subject matter, when we looked at the topics being covered, they were of relatively marginal interest to us given the other priorities which we had at the time. There is also the other issue about how it is going to be taken forward through this centrally funded initiative. We have now started to get some feedback on the earlier joint investment programme, the Force Protection Joint Investment Programme, and that has allowed us to make somewhat of a judgment as to whether or not we should be going forward in this direction. The things which are becoming clear are the Joint Investment Programme. Firstly, it is a model which tends to depend very much on what we would class as financial inputs rather than defence outputs. By defence outputs I mean research which can be exploited for military capability purposes or perhaps can be aligned with a procurement programme. It seems to be based on financial inputs rather than outputs. Somewhat disappointingly as well there is a very heavy management overhead associated with this activity, far greater than we had expected from a programme of equivalent size. Very, very importantly there is the risk of not achieving our national objectives and I will explain what I mean by that. Under the Joint Investment Programme system effectively all the topics are thematic. There is no pre-selection of what work is going to be done before one engages in the programme and can make some money. As a result, nation states who participate do not know whether their research needs are going to be addressed by the particular programme; they may or they may not be, depending on how the programme commences and progresses. However, there is one significant problem and that is that if in whole or in part the needs are not addressed by the Joint Investment Programme we then have to spend more money doing more research,

research we should have done in the first place in order to address our needs. That money has to come from somewhere and has to compete with other high priority needs. In terms of the second part of your question, as to would the rest of Europe benefit, certainly the other nations are free, if they wish, to employ UK firms or UK universities; however, the way the rules have been joined up for the Joint Investment Programme is that it is restricted to those Member States who contribute. A lot of UK expertise would, by the way it is actually constructed, be ruled out. If the UK did actually join the Joint Investment Programme would it benefit the other states? The answer is probably yes. However, if one reversed the question and said would it benefit the UK, I think we would have to say very clearly it would not be of net benefit to the UK.

Q11 Lord Hamilton of Epsom: Are the bilateral things going on here between nation states, between us and European countries, on things of interest to those two countries which, therefore, simplifies the whole thing, mean we are focused on what we really want to do?

Mr Hall: Both in the Force Protection Joint Investment Programme and, to a lesser extent, on this one, the subject matter which is being covered is being covered both nationally and, from the perspective of those parts of it which interest the UK, with other international partners both within and without Europe.

Q12 Lord Anderson of Swansea: It seems a very hard-nosed view. The question of the criteria imposed appears to be: will our own research needs be met and if it does not benefit us we are not going to play even though we will be shutting out our research institutes and universities. Surely smaller nations with smaller research bases could benefit and do we, as a matter of principle, say that we will not participate even though those smaller countries may well benefit and we have much to offer? Clearly partly this depends upon cost. What sort of estimate do we make of the contribution we would make if we did decide to participate?

Mr Hall: In terms of taking your last point first, in terms of the costings they are fairly prescriptive in the Joint Investment Programme system in that the maximum which any country can invest is one third of the total programme and the minimum is 5%.

Q13 Lord Anderson of Swansea: What would we estimate to be our likely cost were we to participate?
Mr Hall: We would not go up to that stage of actually estimating what our cost would be.

Q14 *Lord Anderson of Swansea:* There must be some ball park figures in general. Are we talking of hundreds of thousands?
Mr Hall: I misunderstood the question. The ICET is 15.5 million EUR throughout its life and, therefore, the cost we would incur would be between 5% and 33% of that, so we are looking at up to about 5 million EUR as the cost.

Q15 *Lord Anderson of Swansea*: Over what period?
Mr Hall: Over the two to three year period of the project.

Q16 *Lord Anderson of Swansea:* Less than £1 million a year.
Mr Hall: Yes.

Q17 *Chairman:* How far is this a problem of asymmetry in scale of R&D in Europe in that we have a much higher share of defence R&T than our population share of the European Union presumably?
Mr Hall: It is a very significant factor. Often it is said that research and technology and research and development in Europe is fragmented but we would disagree with that; we would see it as being polarised. If one looks at research and development, 80% or thereabouts is conducted both by France and the UK; the next 10% of the EU is conducted using German funding; the remaining 9% is the Netherlands, Spain, Italy and Sweden with the remainder of the EU nations being 1% or less. That actually sizes the issue quite nicely. We also have done some research looking at the effect of spend on equipment quality which is achieved by research and development and that does show quite a strong stratification within Europe along the lines which I have just mentioned. We have to be very careful not to think that there is more R&T capability in Europe than there actually is. Picking up on one of Lord Anderson's points that I did not quite address, you were talking about working for the benefit of the smaller nations. It is true to say that the smaller nations probably would get benefit from the Joint Investment Programme-type of approach and we would certainly not seek to stop them from engaging together with themselves or with perhaps the more medium-sized nations in doing that. What I would say is we do actually give quite a significant expenditure to Community research and technology more generally under the EU's Research and Development Framework Programme through our contributions to the general EU budget. The totality of that programme is some 50 billion EUR over seven years so I do not think, in any sense, the UK is not doing its bit in supporting European research and development. I think when we do look at military research and technology we have to be aware that of essence it is customer focused, and the customer is military need effectively. You cannot readily apply the models that you do for generalist funding and subsidy of research to the military sphere.

Q18 *Lord Hannay of Chiswick:* Your raising the general R&D framework programme is quite useful because all work that has been done on seven R&D programmes have shown this country benefits a great deal more from these programmes than the amount of money we put in budgetarily because we have a very strong research framework so in a way, you may have got the ball into your own goal. I have dealt with that over many years and that was one of the strong rationales for increasing the R&D spending: this country was a leader in research and did very well out of it. Is there not surely a contradiction between proclaimed policy, which is that we want all the Member States of the European Union to spend more on defence and to be more effective when they spend more, to be more modernised, to be more capable of conducting various missions whether nationally or otherwise—and most of them are members of NATO—and applying a straight zero sum calculation to whether or not we participate in programmes that might enable them to do that?
Mr Hall: I do not think we would necessarily say that for them to be able to increase their military capability means they necessarily need to participate in research and technology programmes. The vast majority of countries in Europe do not have a strong, or in many cases even an existing, defence technology industrial base. One really has to question what use is going to be made of the research which is carried out. My personal assessment is that for many of the countries they would be far better spending the money on what I would call more traditional military applications than on research and technology. The fact is that with the best will in the world they are too small to make a difference at all. In terms of where the major difference would be made, I think it is with the larger countries in Europe who proportionately spend both less on defence and less on defence R&T than the UK and France does. It is perhaps one or two countries in Europe amongst the big six who by increasing their spending on research and technology could make a big difference. It certainly is my assessment that these large multilateral activities are in many respects a distraction from the real issue. If I could pick up on the other point you made about the R&D framework programme, it is very true that certainly in terms of basic research and in terms of cash the UK balance of payments has, in many respects, slightly more money back than it has paid out. Here one has to take into account the UK budget rebate as well when one does that calculation. The trouble is the EU framework programme is essentially a grant-type arrangement similar to the

UK's grant-type arrangement. It is certainly not what we would pass as customer focused research, and research which would be carried out would not be directed towards meeting the needs of the UK military customer. It has more what I would call a subvention tone about it rather than a customer focus.

Q19 *Lord Crickhowell:* I hesitated at the start to come in at this point because we are on the material we look at on the defence package and the scrutiny but I think we can avoid duplication of that because we really have covered pretty effectively and solidly now with Mr Hall's evidence the commentary in paragraph 17, 18 and 19 particularly which has been provided in the Explanatory Memorandum by the Ministry of Defence on that point. It is pretty powerful set of arguments. Following up the point that has just been made, you do say that it is the case that a small number of Member States possess similar technical capabilities to the UK, e.g. in complex weapons, and it is with these countries rather than at an EU level that joint efforts need to be focused to avoid duplication. Furthermore, the pooling of resources suggested by the Commission would tend to draw resources away from national needs and so on. A pretty devastating case seems to be made out in that that has really been repeated by Mr Hall at the present time. The point has just been made that our defence industries might get something more back in terms of finance, but it does seem to me that the case put out in the Memorandum and in Mr Hall's evidence indicates that in terms of defence needs there is an overwhelming case for the concentration where it is in our national interest and by those countries, i.e. the UK and France, whose technical expertise is going to produce the best results. I have tried to avoid having to come back to the issue again because I think the two things taken together we have probably covered what we otherwise have to come back to again later.

Mr Hall: I think that is very true. We would see our support for the EDA as being in terms of the EDA enabling us to co-operate with other nations, small groups of nations, people who have a problem in the same area, in the same way that NATO's Research and Technology Organisation does. NATO does not try to do activities with all of its members, rather it tries to find a sufficient minimum from which to go forward, and I think the minimum is about four members. We have found that that is very powerful in taking forward international collaborative activities.

Q20 *Lord Anderson of Swansea:* Are there some countries which have a niche capability. I am thinking of the Czech Republic and chemical warfare for example, and Slovakia which, in the old days, was very much the heavy end of the Warsaw Pact

capabilities. Do they still retain niche areas which can be built upon in this wider context?

Mr Hall: If I were to be very honest, and I would not want to comment on those countries in particular, I would say we should be very careful not to think that there are some niche centres of excellence throughout Europe which we can somehow synergistically join up. There are some but they tend to be the exception rather than the rule. For instance, although it is outside the EU, Switzerland has a significant capability in what we would call energetic materials, explosives, propellants, etc; however, that tends to be the exception rather than the rule. One has to be cognisant of the fact that there is an enormous stratification in Europe in terms of the capability between those countries which spend the most and those countries who spend relatively little. As I mentioned before, one has to be very careful not to divert resources from things perhaps at which they are good at to things they cannot do so well.

Q21 *Lord Chidgey:* I would like to turn to the concerns over the European Defence Technological and Industrial Base Strategy which you slightly referred to in passing. The Strategy, as I understand it, is currently being drafted and seeks to retain a competitive defence industry in Europe. Can I firstly say whether you would agree with that comment, whether it is a question of retaining a competitive defence industry or establishing a competitive defence industry? Again referring to the Explanatory Memorandum we are coming onto later, in paragraph 2 it makes the point there is a widely held view that the European defence equipment market is not as open or transparent as it should be and that the European Defence Technological and Industrial Base could be more efficient, responsive and competitive, which could be a coded message to say it is not responsive and it is not competitive and it is, as some might suggest, rather stitched up in favour of national interest. The first question is whether or not it is feasible to talk in terms of establishing a competitive defence industry in Europe and does the UK government support this objective. I will come on in a minute to comparisons with our own Defence Industrial Strategy but if you could respond to that question first.

Mr Regan: We have set some of the context for the question in terms of a background of declining defence budgets across Europe. There is, by general agreement, a lot of duplication and protectionism in the existing European defence equipment market. I do not think a European Defence Technology and Industrial Base Strategy as such has an end state of something that is called a competitive European defence industry. What the EDA has done is to identify some of the characteristics that would be associated with a competitive industry and is now working along a number of strands of policy, firstly to give much greater visibility to the nature of the European defence equipment market. This will lead us later into what the European Commission are trying to do with their defence package which is another echo of this issue. From a UK government perspective, we support this work. There is undoubtedly over-capacity and duplication. Mr Hall has given some indication that there are a number of small players but the European defence industry itself, in terms of prime contactors, there are competitive companies but you can probably number them on the fingers of one hand: EADS, BAE Systems, Finmeccanica, Thales and so on and so forth. We do support it and we think it echoes much of the work that we have been trying to do with the Defence Industrial Strategy through things like the electronic bulletin board which the EDA have already established to give visibility of requirements. There is pressure on the application of Article 296, which we will come to in a short time. The final point I think I would make is that it is leading us towards a capability-based approach to the delivery of equipment to the armed forces rather than some of the industrially and economically-based decisions that are a feature of the way some other nations choose to procure their defence equipment.

Q22 *Lord Chidgey:* You have mentioned the comparison with our own Defence Industrial Strategy which is one of the questions I was going to follow with. The DIS is generally accepted and approved across parliament as a very sensible way forward for our defence industry and our defence needs. Now I understand there is some concern about whether that strategy may be under pressure given defence budgets and so forth. It is interesting you should make a comparison with the European Defence Strategy and whether or not there is an equal problem coming up there. The main thrust of my next question is concerning the comment made about one of the benefits of a European Defence Technological and Industrial Base Strategy would be opening up markets in the US. I have to suggest to you that that may be somewhat pie in the sky given the difficulty of penetrating the defence industry in the US. The manner in which our defence industry has been successful is to become established as US companies rather than European companies, talking about BAE Systems of course. Given that background could you perhaps explain to the Committee how the UK's recent award of a contract for the Future Rapid Effects System to an American company relates to the aims of the strategy? It is rather complicated and it does not seem to match any of the policies and aims set out by the European strategy itself or in our response to it.

Mr Regan: Could I deal with your point about the Defence Industrial Strategy first. It was never intended to be a permanent document but was supposed to be, and is, a living document and is in the process of being redrafted. The previous defence equipment minister had a vision that it would be reissued once every two years because it needs to take into account changes in the availability of resources to sustain some of the sectors. With the United States model you are absolutely correct. I spent four years in our Embassy in Washington and there is no doubt that the route to success in selling to the United States is to become a part of the United States defence industry. That is how BAE Systems and Rolls Royce have approached it very successfully in both cases. In terms of FRES, I am in danger of getting into semantics a little. The award of the design contract for FRES has gone to GDUK. In defining what British industry is as a part of a European defence industrial base, we are not so much interested in ownership as in the presence of design authority capability and technology.

Q23 *Lord Chidgey:* White collar rather than blue collar?
Mr Regan: Yes and no, with respect. These vehicles are originally a Swiss design. They will be manufactured, for the most part, in the United Kingdom and we will establish the production facilities here. We have not yet determined which company may assemble or build those vehicles but the main thing is to retain in the UK the design authority, the competence and the intellectual property that will allow us to equip, fit out, maintain and upgrade them on the basis of national operational sovereignty. In our support for the European Defence Industrial Strategy I think I should add a codicil to what I said earlier, which is that the UK will continue to look to the global market for the delivery of equipment capability. There is nothing inherent in a European Defence Technological and Industrial Base, as far as the United Kingdom is concerned, some others may disagree, that automatically points you to the European defence supply market for capability.

Q24 *Lord Hamilton of Epsom:* I should declare an interest. I do work for an American company, way down the food chain, on the FRES programme. Is there any difference between BAE owning a seriously large number of defence companies in the United States and General Dynamics owning GDUK and Lockheed Martin owning Huntings and all the other American majors owning companies over here? In principle does it make any difference?

Mr Regan: In principle I do not think it does make any difference. From the Ministry of Defence perspective we would regard those UK subsidiaries as part of the UK Defence Industrial base.

Q25 *Lord Hamilton of Epsom:* Can we move on to the serious elephant in the room which, when we are talking in European terms, we like to ignore which is the United States of America who are spending more money on defence than we can even dream about. They are increasing their defence budgets year on year by practically the same amount as we spend in one year and spending 35% on research and technology. If we do not actually buy in one way or the other into the United States we are going to be left miles behind if we want our troops to be properly equipped, are we not?

Mr Regan: That is why we default to the global market and why we are involved in programmes like Joint Strike Fighter, for instance. That is where the technology base and the equipment capability that we need can be sourced. From a defence equipment and support perspective, we will go where the best capability can be found. It is not just a question of massive investment but there is also the issue of interoperability because we generally tend to be engaged in coalitions with the United States. That is a factor not only for us but for other European nations as well.

Q26 *Chairman:* Is the parallel, therefore, between our own Defence Industrial Strategy, which enables us to have a capacity here but also our procurement is global, and in the same way the European Defence Technological and Industrial Base is to ensure that there is a capacity within Europe but also with the options for global purchase?

Mr Regan: Absolutely. The overriding factor in those procurement decisions is a reflection of what I said earlier about FRES; the ability autonomously in the United Kingdom to be able to maintain and upgrade those aircraft. We have gone to extraordinary lengths not only with other nations but with the Americans, in particular on Joint Strike Fighter, to ensure we are able to maintain them and have what we term operational sovereignty in our ability to deploy the equipment in the way we see fit and without any hindrance.

Q27 *Chairman:* Were there tough negotiations before we finally agreed the contract in order to maintain that technological advantage to the UK?

Mr Regan: Indeed, yes.

Q28 *Lord Selkirk of Douglas:* Perhaps I should announce that I am an unpaid trustee on one of brother's companies which had a relationship with Lockheed Martin but not on the subject which I am

going to raise with you. You mentioned the subject of helicopters. How optimistic are you that the helicopter availability initiative will make a real difference to improving the availability of helicopters for European security and defence policy operations?

Mr Mathewson: We live in hope and we are going to try is the top line of the answer. There is a problem with the availability of helicopters for demanding military operations. The analysis NATO has conducted shows there are a number of helicopters around; they are not widely available in Afghanistan. In some cases it is the pilots not sufficiently trained, in some cases they are not practising in the hot, dry, dusty conditions, in some cases the helicopters are simply not up to the task and we have identified this as an area we need to work on. We have made a small amount of money available, money which was programmed at end of the last financial year to support peace-keeping operations, and was available as end of year under-spend which we managed to got hold of from the Treasury. Nationally we have put in about 7 million EUR, which has been built up so far to 10 million EUR, with additional contributions from Norway, Iceland and Lithuania. We are still working others to try to get them to contribute. We are identifying solutions, both in the area of training, and we will be inviting interests to come and make a case for access to money for upgrading. We have done quite a bit both in terms of money and in terms of staff time that we have put into this. We are working the issue pretty hard. It does require, at the end of the day, countries actually who have the helicopters wanting to play their part in the project and wanting to commit some of their resources to it as well. If the initiative is simply our 10 million EUR so far, then clearly it does not go very far. We do require the countries with the helicopters or with the pilots who need upgrading to come forward and be willing participants and put some of their own resources into it.

Q29 *Chairman:* We have already touched on it but can we move to the Commission Defence Package and, first of all, the Directive on the coordination of procedures for the award of certain public works contracts or defence works contracts. Could you confirm that is Directive designed to open markets rather than in itself to set up joint procurement programmes?

Mr Regan: Yes, I can confirm that is the case. The objectives I think are twofold: on the one hand, to recognise the peculiarities of defence procurement. It is a means of providing equipment in a way that has some unusual features that are not part of the broader public procurement policy in the existing directive. Secondly, the Commission have long-held reservations about the use of Article 296 of the Treaty which has undoubtedly been abused but I would like to think not by the United Kingdom. There are nations in Europe who invoke Article 296 on grounds of essential interests of national security at all possible opportunities. They are, therefore, providing a framework for process in procurement rather than trying to impose a policy that drives us towards more collaborative programmes. The key really is if there are collaborative programmes which would be brought together by consenting states they will be able to use the provisions of the new Directive to govern them. It is a matter of process rather than policy.

Q30 *Lord Hamilton of Epsom:* Is the whole idea of putting out to competition very major defence contracts completely utopian? If we wanted to get best value for money on our carrier programme, there is an argument you should have it built in the Far East but we all know politics rules here. You have masses of shipbuilding interests all around the country. We are in the farcical position now where these carriers are going to be built in segments in practically every port in England and Scotland and then sailed around to Rosyth for final assembly. It is about the most inefficient way you could build anything. Rather interestingly Rosyth is in the Prime Minister's constituency. What world are we living in? The fact is that it is not an option to have these carriers built abroad, and it must be the same in France, Germany and everywhere else. They have to use, and their governments are expected to use, their own defence industries for major contracts. There is a lot going on in terms of minor contracts. It is quite interesting this document we were given which said there was a tremendous problem with licensing and then they went on to say there are 11,500 licenses issued every year without any difficulty at all. One part of the document contradicted the other. The fact is at a low level below the radar there is business going on across Europe but when it comes to major contracts they will be awarded nationally. How will you ever get away from that?
Mr Regan: There will always be major national defence equipment programmes which are a part of the industrial capability-based approach that any nation would take and that will inevitably remain the case. On the utopian idea of competing major equipment contracts, I agree there is a certain real politick that has to be attendant on that. It can be argued that in terms of the autonomy, as I was saying earlier on the ability to develop, design and maintain equipment, is a part of the framework of operational sovereignty and, therefore, is a legitimate part of the essential interests of national security as defined in Article 296. There is a process, however, that goes beyond that, which is the exposure of the abuses of the system. I have seen examples of Article 296 used to justify national procurement of firemen's helmets.

There is a scale and a horizon across which this business takes place. The Commission recognise that they will not remove Article 296 and that will still be a feature of defence procurement, but they are trying to limit its use. That is the main objective. A part of that is generating better transparency of what is going on in the market.

Q31 *Lord Boyce:* I wonder whether or not you could make a comment on how well the Code of Conduct is operating which was supposed to alleviate some of these problems, Italian wine glasses for officers and so on.
Mr Regan: I have not brought any statistics on the use of the Code of Conduct, however there is a very healthy balance of business which is now being demonstrated. These are contracts which are subject to Article 296 but which are nevertheless available for international procurement. That has been monitored by the EDA and some countries are now starting to be named and shamed in international forums.

Q32 *Chairman:* Is it the case that while we have had relatively good schemes of licensing and have been relatively open in terms of our own market, except for the critical large items to which Lord Hamilton has referred, that is not the case in many other countries and, therefore, it would be to the advantage of the UK industry to the extent that there was an opening up of other people's markets?
Mr Regan: I have to limit my response simply because this is a matter for BERR. However, as a general comment, yes, we have devised an export control system which we think works quite well. I am not expert on the intra-Community Transfer Directive but I think if you read it carefully it shows certain echoes of the UK system which is likely to be adopted in a broader context across Europe.

Q33 *Chairman:* We are more likely to gain from something of this sort.
Mr Regan: We certainly will not lose by it.

Q34 *Lord Jones:* Following on from Lord Roper, and the context in Baroness Taylor's letter of June 18, you know that the government is pursuing the aim of removing the security sector from the scope of the Directive. That, I believe, is inclusive of non-military security purchases. What are the reasons given by the Commission for the inclusion of the security sector in the scope of the Directive, and if the security sector is removed from the scope of the Directive will the MoD and the sector itself still be able to benefit from the specific provisions in the Directive on, for example, security of supply and security of information?

Mr Regan: The UK is in a small minority in the position we have taken, and, under QMV, I would not wish to hold out much hope that we would be ultimately successful. However, the reason why security is included in the scope is because across Europe you will find gendarmeries, carabinieri, Guardia Civil, paramilitary forces which are not technically part of the defence and military structure but which are nevertheless in that security sector where increasingly they operate alongside military forces in overseas operations. The Commission, therefore, believe, supported by the nations that have these paramilitary forces and given that a lot of the equipment they use is similar if not identical to equipment used by the military and defence armed forces, they should be included in the scope of this Directive. From the UK's perspective we see it somewhat differently because we are thinking more in terms of security services than paramilitary forces.

Q35 Lord Jones: Security services being what?
Mr Regan: Intelligence services which brings us into the area of classified contracts which must be retained on a national basis. One of the issues that we are still in discussion with the Commission over is Article 14 of the existing Public Procurement Directive which provides an exemption in those circumstances but which has been removed from the Directive that we are now considering. We are making considerable progress in that negotiation. I think I may be getting ahead of myself slightly. To answer your second point, if we are successful in removing security from the scope then of course we will still be able to use the provisions on security of supply, and security information will still apply to the defence sector.

Q36 Lord Boyce: Understandably the government expressed some concerns in the EM about the Directive in relation to security of information and whether one would get into the ECJ taking a stance on what could be perceived as interfering with the national and Member States' own ability to make its own decisions and also the deletion of the research and development exemption. Since the EM was written has there been any progress in resolving some of those issues?
Mr Regan: Yes, we have expressed our concern. There are now new security of information provisions. We have been successful in getting references to some aspects into the recitals and to some of the early articles. We are still working to get a more explicit recognition of the need to have security of information explicitly included, i.e. that would be reciting Article 14 from the Public Procurement Directive. As far as the potential for involvement of the ECJ is concerned, I think we are so far being successful in limiting that aspect of it. However, the Commission have already indicated,

and they will stand by their intention, to refer what they consider to be abuses of Article 296 to the ECJ in a more proactive and vigorous way than has been the case hitherto. The ECJ will, I suspect, still be playing a more prominent role but perhaps not so much in the area of security of information.

Q37 Lord Boyce: Are we concerned that the ECJ will try to make decisions on what would be considered to be issues of national security on our part?
Mr Regan: We have been successful in modifying the language. This is very much work in progress. The negotiation continues but we have been successful in getting some recognition of this into the document and we have produced alternative wording should we be unsuccessful in replicating the exemption that is currently in Article 14 of the Public Procurement Directive. We will see where this goes under the French presidency but they are quite keen that they should complete work on this in the course of their presidency of the EU. We are looking now towards a fairly vigorous continuation of these negotiations.

Q38 Lord Boyce: What about the research and development exemption?
Mr Regan: We are looking at the wording that the Commission have proposed on research and development exemptions which is still a matter of discussion. We are consulting with lawyers as to the precise subtleties and nuances of the language that the Commission have provided. Some of this they are taking back to reconsider, and I should add that on security scope one of the issues that the Commission are starting to discover is that some of these definitions—and we have had something of this debate this morning on what does security mean— they are having to go back not necessarily to the drawing board but certainly they are going to be shading some of the drawings.

Q39 Chairman: In terms of the timetable, you were just talking about completion during the French presidency but you do not see this as happening early in the French presidency.
Mr Regan: No.
Chairman: We need to take that into account in terms of clearing the documents if you are pleading inclusion.

Q40 Lord Crickhowell: If we turn to Battlegroups, earlier in the summer Lord Hamilton and I, and our special adviser and clerk, visited Warminster and had a look at the Battlegroup in operation. I asked Brigadier Butler, who sadly has announced his decision to leave the Army, the obvious question about our ability to deploy the Battlegroup in the second half of 2008 in view of our commitments elsewhere. He gave a suitably diplomatic and military answer but I think that both Lord Hamilton and I came away with a big question mark hanging over the situation reinforced by the increasing pressure since. Would you like to give me an answer as to how capable you think we will be of deploying a Battlegroup if the pressures we are under elsewhere continue?

Mr Mathewson: It was good to see you and Lord Hamilton at the exercise and you will have seen that the preparations for the Battlegroup are serious. There is no doubt that we are taking our commitment seriously. The training was of a very high quality and the planning has been conducted seriously. You will probably accuse me, like Brigadier Butler, of giving you a diplomatic answer to your question which is that our preparations are serious. The Battlegroup is available. We have the capacity to deploy it and to scale it for whatever mission is required with the capabilities but clearly the government will have to take a careful view at the time on competing demands. The Battlegroup is found from our Joint Rapid Reaction Force and there may, at the time, be competing demands on the Joint Rapid Reaction Force. The fact that it is drawn from the Joint Rapid Reaction Force means that it is not a force which is earmarked for Iraq or Afghanistan but we all know that contingencies arise that we have not foreseen and there may be national demands on the JRRF which we have not foreseen. I can only say this would be a matter for decision at the time but that the capability is serious and available subject to those pressures.

Q41 *Lord Crickhowell:* You will recall, as we watched the Royal Fusiliers operation in the afternoon, we heard that they had all been involved in almost every operation that one could think of in an intensive way over the previous five years and, therefore, one is only too acutely aware that if they did happen to deploy them it would be adding yet another of the excessive burdens that those individuals have had to bear over quite a long time.

Mr Mathewson: Yes, indeed. The battalion has been very active and it will be active again in the future. Its role at the moment is to be one of the ready battalions on the JRRF and they are available whether for a national contingency or an EU contingency. I can only say that the government would take these factors into account on any decision on the use of the Battlegroup, bearing in mind also there is a second Battlegroup on standby alongside the British Battlegroup.

Q42 *Chairman:* Could I ask, in very general terms, as to whether the evacuation of European nationals from a difficult situation, a possible ESDP operation, could be undertaken by Battlegroup?

Mr Mathewson: Yes, that is just the sort of thing which conceptually could be undertaken by the Battlegroup.

Q43 *Chairman:* I would like to ask our last question and come back, in one sense, to EDA and the role of the EDA as defined in the Lisbon Treaty. If the Treaty were to enter into force it would give the EDA a specific legal basis in the EU's primary law and it would also, to some extent, enlarge its mandate. If the Treaty does not come into force, do you see this in any way as undermining the continuing authority and legitimacy of the European Defence Agency?

Mr Mathewson: No, we do not. The EDA operates now perfectly adequately on the basis of the joint action adopted in 2004. This is a legally binding decision. No, is the short answer. We see it continuing to operate perfectly adequately on the basis of its current joint action.

Chairman: Mr Mathewson, can I thank you and Mr Regan and Mr Hall for having come and taken such a wide range of questions from us. We have found it very useful and it helps us in our consideration of the various matters which do come before us in the areas for which we are responsible.

ISBN 978-0-10-401343-4

9 780104 013434